THE CREDIT CARD BIBLE

EVERYTHING YOU NEED TO KNOW TO USE CREDIT CARDS

ANURAG YADAV

Copyright © Anurag Yadav
All Rights Reserved.

This book has been self-published with all reasonable efforts taken to make the material error-free by the author. No part of this book shall be used, reproduced in any manner whatsoever without written permission from the author, except in the case of brief quotations embodied in critical articles and reviews.

The Author of this book is solely responsible and liable for its content including but not limited to the views, representations, descriptions, statements, information, opinions and references ["Content"]. The Content of this book shall not constitute or be construed or deemed to reflect the opinion or expression of the Publisher or Editor. Neither the Publisher nor Editor endorse or approve the Content of this book or guarantee the reliability, accuracy or completeness of the Content published herein and do not make any representations or warranties of any kind, express or implied, including but not limited to the implied warranties of merchantability, fitness for a particular purpose. The Publisher and Editor shall not be liable whatsoever for any errors, omissions, whether such errors or omissions result from negligence, accident, or any other cause or claims for loss or damages of any kind, including without limitation, indirect or consequential loss or damage arising out of use, inability to use, or about the reliability, accuracy or sufficiency of the information contained in this book.

Made with ♥ on the Notion Press Platform
www.notionpress.com

Contents

Foreword   *vii*

Acknowledgements   *ix*

1. Credit Card Savvy For Beginners   1

Understanding What A Credit Card Is And How It Works

The Benefits And Drawbacks Of Using A Credit Card

How Credit Cards Differ From Other Forms Of Credit

2. Get Your Credit Card In India: A Step-by-step Guide   9

The Documentation And Eligibility Requirements For Applying For A Credit Card In India

How To Compare Different Credit Card Offers And Choose The Best One For You

Tips For Successfully Completing A Credit Card Application

3. Credit Card Jungle: Sorting Through The Options In India   19

Cashback Credit Cards

Travel Credit Cards

Rewards Credit Cards

Premium Credit Cards

Secured Credit Cards

Student Credit Cards

4. Understanding Credit Card Fees And Charges   35

Annual Fees, Interest Rates, And Other Charges To Watch Out For

How To Avoid Or Minimize Credit Card Fees

How To Read And Understand Your Credit Card Statement

5. The Smart Way To Use Credit Cards   43

Contents

How To Set A Budget And Stick To It When Using Your Credit Card

How To Avoid Overspending And Racking Up Credit Card Debt

How To Build And Maintain A Good Credit History

6. Credit Card Debt Demolition: Proven Strategies For   53
   Paying It Off

Strategies For Paying Down Credit Card Debt

How To Negotiate With Your Credit Card Issuer To Reduce Or Eliminate Fees Or Interest

How To Work With A Credit Counselor Or Debt Management Service

7. How To Dispute A Charge On Your Credit Card   65

What To Do If You Spot An Unauthorized Charge On Your Credit Card Statement

How To File A Dispute With Your Credit Card Issuer

What To Expect During The Dispute Resolution Process

8. Fraud Prevention Pro: Mastering The Art Of Credit Card   75
   Security

How To Spot And Report Credit Card Fraud

Tips For Keeping Your Credit Card Information Safe Online And Offline

How To Recover From Credit Card Fraud

9. The Ultimate Credit Boost: Proven Strategies For   87
   Improving Your Score

What Goes Into Your Credit Score And How To Improve It

How To Check Your Credit Report And Dispute Errors

Contents

How To Rebuild Your Credit After A Financial Setback

10. Clearing The Credit Haze: Answering Common   97
    Questions On Indian Credit Cards

Can You Have More Than One Credit Card In India?'.

How To Report A Lost Or Stolen Credit Card In India?

How To Close A Credit Card Account In India?

How To Check Credit Card Balance And Transaction History In India?

What Happens When You Don't Pay Credit Card Bill In India?

Conclusion   109

Last Word   111

Foreword

As we move into an increasingly digital world, credit cards have become an integral part of our financial lives. They offer convenience, flexibility, and rewards, but they also come with risks and responsibilities. This guide is an in-depth look at the ins and outs of using credit cards in India, starting with an introduction to credit cards and their uses, and moving on to the benefits and drawbacks of using a credit card. It also explains how credit cards differ from other forms of credit and provides detailed information on the documentation and eligibility requirements for applying for a credit card in India. Additionally, it covers tips for comparing different credit card offers and choosing the best one for you, as well as strategies for using credit cards responsibly. The guide also provides information on credit card fees and charges, how to read and understand your credit card statement, and tips for managing and paying off credit card debt. Additionally, it covers how to dispute a charge on your credit card, how to protect yourself from credit card fraud, and how to improve your credit score. The guide concludes with frequently asked questions about using credit cards in India, including how to check credit card balance and transaction history, how to close a credit card account, and what happens when you don't pay a credit card bill.

This guide is a valuable resource for anyone looking to use credit cards responsibly and make informed decisions about credit in India. Whether you're a first-time credit card user or a seasoned pro, this guide offers valuable insights and practical advice that will help you navigate the world of credit cards with confidence. It is my hope that this guide will empower you to make the most of your credit card and achieve your financial goals.

Acknowledgements

I would like to express my gratitude to all those who have contributed to the creation of this guide on using credit cards in India. This guide would not have been possible without the valuable insights and expertise of financial experts and credit card industry professionals. I would also like to thank the research team who have put in countless hours of effort to gather and verify the information presented in this guide.

Lastly, I would like to thank all the readers who have taken the time to read this guide. I hope that it proves to be a valuable resource for anyone looking to use credit cards responsibly and make informed decisions about credit in India.

CREDIT CARD SAVVY FOR BEGINNERS

Understanding what a credit card is and how it works

A credit card is a financial instrument that allows individuals to borrow money from a financial institution, known as the issuer, in order to make purchases or withdraw cash. The issuer extends a line of credit to the cardholder, which can be used to make purchases or withdraw cash up to a certain limit. The cardholder is then responsible for repaying the borrowed amount, plus any interest or fees that may be charged, according to the terms of the cardholder agreement.

When a cardholder makes a purchase with a credit card, the merchant submits the transaction to the issuer for approval. The issuer then checks the cardholder's creditworthiness and available credit to determine whether to approve or decline the transaction. If the transaction is approved, the issuer pays the merchant and the cardholder is responsible for repaying the issuer, either in full or in minimum payments.

There are many different types of credit cards, each with its own set of features and benefits. Some common types of credit cards include:

Revolving credit cards: These cards allow the cardholder to carry a balance from month to month, with interest charged on the outstanding balance.

Charge cards: These cards require the cardholder to pay the balance in full each month, with no interest charged.

Secured credit cards: These cards require the cardholder to make a security deposit in order to establish credit.

Prepaid credit cards: These cards are pre-loaded with a certain amount of funds and can be used like a debit card, but the user will not be able to use more than the amount loaded on the card.

Credit cards can be a useful tool for managing finances and building credit, but they can also be dangerous if not used responsibly. It's important to understand the terms and conditions of a credit card, including the interest rate, fees, and rewards program, before applying for one. It is also essential to understand that if you don't pay your credit card bill on time, it will negatively affect your credit score, and you may end up incurring late payment charges, penalty charges, and high-interest rates.

It's also important to be aware of the risks of credit card fraud and identity theft, and take steps to protect yourself. This includes monitoring your credit card statements regularly, using strong passwords, and being cautious about sharing personal information online.

In conclusion, understanding how a credit card works is crucial for making informed decisions about how to use it. It is important to use credit cards wisely, and be aware of the terms and conditions, risks, and benefits of using a credit card. By being responsible and understanding the mechanics of a credit card, you can avoid many of the common pitfalls and enjoy the benefits that credit cards can provide.

The benefits and drawbacks of using a credit card

Credit cards offer many benefits to consumers, including convenience, building credit, and rewards programs.

One of the main benefits of using a credit card is convenience. Credit cards allow consumers to make purchases without having to carry cash or write a check. They also allow for easy tracking of expenses, as all transactions are recorded on a monthly statement. Additionally, many credit cards offer additional services such as rental car insurance, travel insurance, and purchase protection.

Another benefit of using credit cards is the ability to build credit. A credit card can be a great tool for building credit history, as long as it is used responsibly. When you use a credit card and make payments on time, you demonstrate to lenders that you are a responsible borrower, which can lead to better credit scores and lower interest rates on loans in the future.

Rewards programs are another benefit of using credit cards. Many credit cards offer rewards such as cash back, points, or miles that can be redeemed for merchandise, travel, or statement credits. This can be a great way to save money on everyday expenses or even travel.

However, credit cards also have some drawbacks. One of the main drawbacks of using a credit card is the potential for high-interest rates. If you carry a balance from month to month, the interest charges can add up quickly and make it difficult to pay off the debt. Additionally, if you miss a payment or make a late payment, you may incur additional fees or penalties.

Another drawback of using a credit card is the potential for overspending. It can be easy to overspend when using a credit card, as the sense of immediacy and physicality of cash is not present. This can lead to high levels of credit card debt and financial difficulty.

Credit card fraud is another drawback of using credit cards. It is important to safeguard your credit card information, as it can be vulnerable to theft or misuse by fraudsters.

Finally, credit card companies are businesses and they are in the business of making money. They use different methods such as hidden fees, fine prints, and other tricks to make money from their customers. It is important to be aware of these practices, and read the terms and conditions carefully before applying for or using a credit card.

In conclusion, credit cards offer many benefits, including convenience, building credit, and rewards programs. However, credit cards also have drawbacks, such as high-interest rates, overspending, fraud and hidden fees. It's important to be aware of the risks and rewards of using a credit card, and use them responsibly. By understanding the benefits and drawbacks of using a credit card, consumers can make informed decisions about how to use credit cards to their advantage.

How credit cards differ from other forms of credit

Credit cards are a type of revolving credit, which means that the cardholder can borrow money up to a certain limit and carry a balance from month to month, with interest charged on the outstanding balance. However, credit cards differ from other forms of credit in a number of ways.

One of the main differences between credit cards and other forms of credit is the type of credit extended. A credit card is an unsecured line of credit, which means that the cardholder is not required to put up collateral in order to obtain the credit. In contrast, other forms of credit such as personal loans or mortgages are typically secured, meaning that the borrower must put up collateral such as a home or car in order to obtain the credit.

Another difference between credit cards and other forms of credit is the way in which the credit is used. Credit cards are typically used for everyday purchases such as gas, groceries, and clothing. In contrast, other forms of credit such as personal loans or mortgages are typically used for larger expenses such as buying a house or paying for a medical procedure.

The credit limits on credit cards are generally lower compared to other forms of credit. Credit cards have a revolving limit, which means that the limit changes based on the cardholder's creditworthiness and payment history. In contrast, other forms of credit such as personal loans or mortgages have a fixed limit, which is determined by the lender based on the borrower's creditworthiness and the value of the collateral.

The repayment terms also differ between credit cards and other forms of credit. Credit cards typically require the cardholder to make a minimum payment each month, with interest charged on the outstanding balance. Other forms of credit such as personal loans or mortgages typically require the borrower to make fixed payments over a set period of time, with interest charged on the outstanding balance.

Finally, the interest rates for credit cards are typically higher compared to other forms of credit. Credit card companies charge higher interest rates because credit cards are unsecured loans and the risk of default is higher. In contrast, other forms of credit such as personal loans or mortgages typically have lower interest rates because they are secured loans and the risk of default is lower.

In conclusion, credit cards differ from other forms of credit in a number of ways, including the type of credit extended, the way in which the credit is used, the credit limits, repayment terms and the interest rates. Understanding these differences can help consumers make informed decisions about which form of credit is best for them. It is important to consider the terms and conditions, fees, and interest rates of credit cards and other forms of credit before applying for them.

CHAPTER TWO

GET YOUR CREDIT CARD IN INDIA: A STEP-BY-STEP GUIDE

The documentation and eligibility requirements for applying for a credit card in India

When applying for a credit card in India, there are certain documentation and eligibility requirements that must be met. These requirements vary depending on the type of credit card and the issuer, but generally include proof of identity, proof of income, and credit history.

Proof of identity is typically required when applying for a credit card in India. This can include government-issued identification such as a passport, PAN card, driver's license or voter ID card. Some credit card issuers may also require additional proof of identity, such as a utility bill or rental agreement.

Proof of income is also typically required when applying for a credit card in India. This can include salary slips, bank statement, or income tax returns. Some credit card issuers may also require additional proof of income such as an employer's letter, financial statements, and other documents that can show your income.

In addition to proof of identity and income, credit history is also taken into consideration when applying for a credit card in India. This includes your credit score, payment history, and any outstanding debts. Credit card issuers will check your credit history to determine your creditworthiness and the level of risk involved in extending credit to you.

Eligibility criteria for credit card application in India generally require the applicant to be of legal age and hold a stable source of income. Some credit card issuer's may require a minimum income threshold to be eligible for the card.

It's also important to note that certain credit cards may have specific requirements or criteria that must be met in order to be eligible for the card. For example, a travel credit card may require the applicant to have a certain number of frequent flyer miles, or a premium credit card may require a high income or a high net worth.

In conclusion, applying for a credit card in India requires meeting certain documentation and eligibility requirements. These requirements include proof of identity, proof of income, and credit history. It's important to gather all the required documentation and make sure you meet the eligibility criteria before applying for a credit card. It's also important to understand that certain credit cards may have specific requirements or criteria that must be met in order to be eligible for the card. Being well-informed and prepared before applying for a credit card can increase the chances of approval and help to ensure a smooth application process. Additionally, it's important to compare different credit cards offered by various issuers and select the one that best suits your financial needs and goals. This will help to ensure that you are getting the best deal and the most benefits from your credit card.

It's also important to be mindful of the interest rate, fees and rewards associated with different credit cards. Some credit cards may have a higher interest rate, but may also offer more rewards and benefits. It's important to weigh the pros and cons of each card and select the one that best suits your financial needs and goals.

Furthermore, it's important to read and understand the terms and conditions of the credit card agreement before signing up. This will help you to be aware of the fees, penalties, and other charges that may be associated with the card and make an informed decision.

In summary, applying for a credit card in India requires meeting certain documentation and eligibility requirements. It is important to gather all the required documents, understand the eligibility criteria, compare different credit cards offered by various issuers, and read and understand the terms and conditions of the credit card agreement before signing up. By being well-informed and prepared, you can increase your chances of approval and ensure a smooth application process.

How to compare different credit card offers and choose the best one for you

When comparing different credit card offers, it's important to consider a variety of factors to determine which card is the best fit for you.

One of the first things to consider is the interest rate. The interest rate on a credit card can have a significant impact on the overall cost of credit, so it's important to compare the interest rates of different cards and choose the one with the lowest rate. It's also important to note that some credit cards may offer a low introductory rate, but then increase the rate after a certain period of time.

Another important factor to consider is the rewards program. Many credit cards offer rewards such as cash back, points, or miles for purchases made with the card. It's important to compare the rewards programs of different cards and choose the one that offers the best rewards for your spending habits. For example, if you travel frequently, a card with a travel rewards program may be a better fit for you than a card with a cash-back rewards program.

It's also important to consider the fees associated with different credit cards. Some cards may have annual fees, balance transfer fees, cash advance fees, and other charges. It's important to compare the fees of different cards and choose the one with the lowest fees, or the one whose benefits outweighs the fees.

Another important factor to consider is the credit limit. Some credit cards may have a higher credit limit than others, which can be helpful if you anticipate making large purchases. It's important to consider the credit limit of different cards and choose the one with the highest credit limit that you are comfortable with.

Additional benefits such as travel insurance, purchase protection, and extended warranty are also important to consider. These benefits can provide added protection and savings, so it's important to compare the additional benefits offered by different cards and choose the one that offers the best benefits for you.

It's also important to consider the issuer and customer service. Look for credit card issuer with good reputation, and have a reliable customer service in case you have any issues or concerns.

In conclusion, when comparing different credit card offers, it's important to consider the interest rate, rewards program, fees, credit limit, additional benefits, and the issuer's reputation.

Tips for successfully completing a credit card application

When applying for a credit card, it's important to take the necessary steps to ensure that your application is complete and accurate in order to increase your chances of approval.

One of the first things to do is to gather all the necessary documentation. This includes proof of identity, proof of income, and credit history. Make sure that you have all the required documents ready before you start the application process.

Before filling out the application, you should also research different credit card offers and compare the interest rates, rewards programs, fees, and other features. This will help you to choose the best credit card for your needs and increase your chances of approval.

It's also important to be honest and accurate when filling out the application. Misrepresenting information on a credit card application can result in rejection or even legal action. Be sure to fill out the application completely and accurately, including your income, employment information, and any outstanding debts.

Additionally, it's important to pay attention to the fine print and read the terms and conditions of the credit card agreement before signing up. This will help you to understand the fees, penalties, and other charges associated with the card and make an informed decision.

It's also a good idea to check your credit score before applying for a credit card. This will give you an idea of your creditworthiness and the level of risk involved in extending credit to you. Knowing your credit score will also help you to identify and address any issues that may be affecting your creditworthiness.

When submitting the application, it's also important to be patient. The credit card issuer will need to verify your information and check your credit history before making a decision. It may take several days or even a few weeks for the issuer to process your application.

Finally, it's important to monitor your credit card statements and credit report regularly. This will help you to catch any errors or fraudulent.

CHAPTER THREE

CREDIT CARD JUNGLE: SORTING THROUGH THE OPTIONS IN INDIA

Cashback credit cards

Cashback credit cards are a type of credit card that rewards cardholders with cash back on their purchases. This cash back can be redeemed for statement credits, merchandise, or other rewards.

One of the main benefits of cashback credit cards is the ability to earn cash back on everyday purchases. Many cashback credit cards offer a certain percentage of cash back on all purchases, while others offer higher cash back rates on specific categories of purchases such as groceries, gas, or travel. This can be a great way to save money on everyday expenses.

Another benefit of cashback credit cards is that they can help to offset the cost of interest. If you carry a balance from month to month, the cash back earned can help to offset the interest charges. This can make it easier to pay off the debt over time.

Cashback credit cards also offer a variety of redemption options. Some cards allow cardholders to redeem cash back for statement credits, while others offer the option to redeem for merchandise or travel. Some cards also allow you to transfer your cashback rewards to other loyalty programs such as airline frequent-flyer programs.

When choosing a cashback credit card, it's important to compare the cashback rewards offered by different cards. Some cards offer a flat rate of cash back on all purchases, while others offer higher cash back rates on specific categories of purchases. It's also important to consider the annual fee, interest rate, and other fees associated with the card.

It's also important to read the terms and conditions of the credit card agreement before signing up. This will help you to understand the rules regarding earning and redeeming cashback rewards, and any restrictions or limitations that may apply.

Another important factor to consider is the minimum redemption threshold. Some cards require cardholders to accumulate a certain amount of cashback before they can redeem their rewards. This means that you may have to wait longer to redeem your rewards if you don't have a high spending rate.

It's also important to consider the expiration date of the rewards. Some cards have expiration date for the rewards, after that date the rewards will no longer be valid. This means that you'll need to use the rewards before they expire or they'll be forfeited.

In conclusion, cashback credit cards are a great way to save money on everyday purchases. They offer cardholders the ability to earn cash back on their purchases, which can be redeemed for statement credits, merchandise, or other rewards. When choosing a cashback credit card, it's important to compare the cashback rewards offered by different cards, consider the annual fee, interest rate, and other fees associated with the card, and read the terms and conditions of the credit card agreement. Additionally, consider the minimum redemption threshold, expiration date of the rewards and other terms and conditions before signing up for a cashback credit card.

Travel credit cards

Travel credit cards are a type of credit card that rewards cardholders with points, miles, or other rewards for purchases made with the card. These rewards can then be redeemed for travel-related expenses such as flights, hotels, and rental cars.

One of the main benefits of travel credit cards is the ability to earn rewards for travel-related expenses. Many travel credit cards offer a high rewards rate for purchases made with the card. These rewards can be used to book flights, hotels, rental cars, and other travel-related expenses. This can help to offset the cost of travel, making it more affordable.

Another benefit of travel credit cards is the ability to earn rewards on everyday purchases. Many travel credit cards offer a high rewards rate on all purchases, which can help to earn rewards quickly. Additionally, many cards offer bonus rewards on specific categories such as dining, supermarkets and groceries.

Travel credit cards also offer a variety of redemption options. Some cards allow cardholders to redeem rewards for flights on any airline, while others are tied to a specific airline or hotel chain. Some cards offer the flexibility to transfer rewards to other loyalty programs such as airline frequent-flyer programs or hotel loyalty programs.

When choosing a travel credit card, it's important to compare the rewards offered by different cards. Some cards offer a flat rate of rewards on all purchases, while others offer higher rewards rates on specific categories of purchases such as travel or dining. It's also important to consider the annual fee, interest rate, and other fees associated with the card.

It's also important to read the terms and conditions of the credit card agreement before signing up. This will help you to understand the rules regarding earning and redeeming rewards, and any restrictions or limitations that may apply.

Another important factor to consider is the expiration date of the rewards. Some cards have expiration date for the rewards, after that date the rewards will no longer be valid. This means that you'll need to use the rewards before they expire or they'll be forfeited.

Another thing to consider is the blackout dates, some rewards program have specific dates that the rewards cannot be used, this can limit the flexibility of your trip planning.

Finally, it's important to consider the additional benefits offered by the card. Some travel credit cards offer benefits such as travel insurance, trip cancellation coverage, and rental car insurance. These benefits can provide added protection and savings while traveling.

In conclusion, travel credit cards are a great way to earn rewards for travel-related expenses. They offer cardholders the ability to earn rewards on everyday purchases and redeem them for flights, hotels, rental cars, and other travel-related expenses. When choosing a travel credit card, it's important to compare the rewards offered by different cards, consider the annual fee, interest rate, and other fees associated with the card, and read the terms and conditions of the credit card agreement. Additionally, consider the expiration date of the rewards, blackout dates, additional benefits and other terms and conditions before signing up for a travel credit card.

Rewards credit cards

Rewards credit cards are a type of credit card that rewards cardholders with points, cashback, or other rewards for purchases made with the card. These rewards can then be redeemed for a variety of items such as merchandise, statement credits, travel, or gift cards.

One of the main benefits of rewards credit cards is the ability to earn rewards on everyday purchases. Many rewards credit cards offer a high rewards rate for purchases made with the card, which can help to earn rewards quickly. Additionally, many cards offer bonus rewards on specific categories such as dining, supermarkets, gas and groceries.

Another benefit of rewards credit cards is the flexibility in redemption options. Many rewards credit cards offer a wide range of redemption options such as statement credits, merchandise, travel, and gift cards. Some cards also allow you to transfer your rewards to other loyalty programs such as airline frequent-flyer programs or hotel loyalty programs.

When choosing a rewards credit card, it's important to compare the rewards offered by different cards. Some cards offer a flat rate of rewards on all purchases, while others offer higher rewards rates on specific categories of purchases. It's also important to consider the annual fee, interest rate, and other fees associated with the card.

It's also important to read the terms and conditions of the credit card agreement before signing up. This will help you to understand the rules regarding earning and redeeming rewards, and any restrictions or limitations that may apply.

Another important factor to consider is the expiration date of the rewards. Some cards have expiration date for the rewards, after that date the rewards will no longer be valid. This means that you'll need to use the rewards before they expire or they'll be forfeited.

It's also important to consider the minimum redemption threshold. Some cards require cardholders to accumulate a certain amount of rewards before they can redeem them. This means that you may have to wait longer to redeem your rewards if you don't have a high spending rate.

Finally, it's important to consider the additional benefits offered by the card. Some rewards credit cards offer benefits such as purchase protection, extended warranty, and travel insurance. These benefits can provide added protection and savings.

In conclusion, rewards credit cards are a great way to earn rewards on everyday purchases. They offer cardholders the ability to earn rewards and redeem them for a variety of items such as merchandise, statement credits, travel, or gift cards. When choosing a rewards credit card, it's important to compare the rewards offered by different cards, consider the annual fee, interest rate, and other fees associated with the card, and read the terms and conditions of the credit card agreement. Additionally, consider the expiration date of the rewards, minimum redemption threshold, additional benefits and other terms and conditions before signing up for a rewards credit card.

Premium credit cards

Premium credit cards are a type of credit card that is designed for high-income individuals with excellent credit. These cards typically come with higher credit limits, exclusive benefits, and superior rewards programs.

One of the main benefits of premium credit cards is the high credit limit. These cards often come with credit limits that are significantly higher than those of standard credit cards. This can be helpful for those who plan to make large purchases or need to carry a balance from month to month.

Another benefit of premium credit cards is the exclusive benefits and perks that they offer. Many premium credit cards come with benefits such as airport lounge access, concierge services, travel insurance, and purchase protection. Some cards also offer exclusive access to events and experiences such as concerts, sporting events, and VIP experiences.

Premium credit cards also offer superior rewards programs. Many premium credit cards offer higher rewards rates and more generous rewards than standard credit cards. They also often offer a wider range of redemption options and more flexibility when it comes to redeeming rewards.

When choosing a premium credit card, it's important to compare the rewards and benefits offered by different cards. It's also important to consider the annual fee, interest rate, and other fees associated with the card.

It's also important to read the terms and conditions of the credit card agreement before signing up. This will help you to understand the rules regarding earning and redeeming rewards, and any restrictions or limitations that may apply.

Another important factor to consider is the minimum spend required to qualify for the rewards or benefits. Some premium credit cards require cardholders to spend a certain amount in order to qualify for the rewards or benefits offered. This means that you may have to spend more than you typically would in order to earn rewards or access benefits.

It's also important to consider the additional fees associated with the card such as foreign transaction fees, balance transfer fees, and cash advance fees. These fees can add up quickly and can significantly impact the overall cost of credit.

Finally, it's important to consider the customer service and issuer's reputation. Look for a credit card issuer with a good reputation, and have a reliable customer service in case you have any issues or concerns.

In conclusion, premium credit cards are a type of credit card that is designed for high-income individuals with excellent credit. They offer high credit limits, exclusive benefits, superior rewards programs, and often come with higher annual fees. When choosing a premium credit card, it's important to compare the rewards and benefits offered by different cards, consider the annual fee, interest rate, and other fees associated with the card, read the terms and conditions of the credit card agreement and consider the issuer's reputation and customer service before signing up. Additionally, consider the minimum spend required to qualify for the rewards or benefits, additional fees and other terms and conditions associated with the card before signing up.

Secured credit cards

Secured credit cards are a type of credit card that is designed for individuals with limited or poor credit. They are called "secured" because they require a security deposit to be made before the card is issued. The deposit acts as collateral for the credit card, and is typically equal to the credit limit.

One of the main benefits of secured credit cards is that they are easier to obtain than traditional credit cards. They are often a good option for individuals who have limited or poor credit and have been denied for a traditional credit card. They can help to build or improve credit history, as long as the cardholder makes on-time payments and keeps their balance low.

Another benefit of secured credit cards is that they offer the opportunity to increase credit limit. Once the cardholder has demonstrated responsible use of the card, many issuers will consider increasing the credit limit. This can help to improve the credit score and also increase the purchasing power.

Secured credit cards also offer a variety of benefits, such as rewards programs, cashback, or other incentives. This can be a great way to earn rewards while also building or improving credit history.

When choosing a secured credit card, it's important to compare the fees, interest rates and other terms and conditions associated with the card. Some secured credit cards may have high fees, high-interest rates, or other unfavorable terms. It's also important to read the terms and conditions of the credit card agreement before signing up.

Another important factor to consider is the refund policy of the security deposit. Some issuers may have a policy of refunding the deposit after a certain period of time, while others may only refund it if the account is closed in good standing. It's important to understand the issuer's policy before applying for a secured credit card, to ensure that you will be able to get your deposit back if you decide to close the account or upgrade to a traditional credit card.

It's also important to consider the reporting of the credit information to the credit bureaus. Not all secured credit cards report to all three major credit bureaus, so it's important to check with the issuer to see if they report to the bureaus that you want to improve your credit score with.

Another thing to consider is the conversion option. Some issuers may have an option to convert the secured credit card to an unsecured credit card after a certain period of time. This can be a great way to upgrade to a traditional credit card and have the security deposit refunded.

It's also important to manage your credit card responsibly. This means making on-time payments, keeping your balance low, and avoiding unnecessary fees and interest charges. By managing your credit card responsibly, you can build or improve your credit history and increase your chances of being approved for a traditional credit card in the future.

In conclusion, secured credit cards are a type of credit card that is designed for individuals with limited or poor credit. They require a security deposit to be made before the card is issued, which acts as collateral for the credit card. They can help to build or improve credit history, offer the opportunity to increase credit limit, offer various benefits such as rewards programs, cashback, or other incentives and are easier to obtain than traditional credit cards. When choosing a secured credit card, it's important to compare the fees, interest rates, terms and conditions, refund policy, reporting of credit information to credit bureaus, conversion option, the issuer's reputation and customer service before signing up. Additionally, it's important to manage the credit card responsibly in order to build or improve your credit history and increase your chances of being approved for a traditional credit card in the future.

Student credit cards

Student credit cards are a type of credit card specifically designed for college students who are looking to establish a credit history. They are designed to help students build credit and learn responsible credit card use while they are still in school.

One of the main benefits of student credit cards is that they can help students build credit. Many student credit cards are designed to help students establish a credit history, which can be beneficial when they are ready to apply for a traditional credit card or a loan after graduation.

Another benefit of student credit cards is that they come with lower credit limits, which can help to reduce the risk of students getting into serious debt. Additionally, many student credit cards come with educational resources and tools to help students understand credit and how to use it responsibly.

Student credit cards also offer rewards programs, cashback, or other incentives. This can be a great way to earn rewards while also building or improving credit history.

When choosing a student credit card, it's important to compare the fees, interest rates, and other terms and conditions associated with the card. Some student credit cards may have high fees, high-interest rates, or other unfavorable terms. It's also important to read the terms and conditions of the credit card agreement before signing up.

Another important factor to consider is the reporting of the credit information to the credit bureaus. Not all student credit cards report to all three major credit bureaus, so it's important to check with the issuer to see if they report to the bureaus that you want to improve your credit score with.

It's also important to consider the issuer's policy regarding co-signers. Some issuers may require a co-signer for students who do not have a credit history or income.

CHAPTER FOUR

UNDERSTANDING CREDIT CARD FEES AND CHARGES

Annual fees, Interest rates, and other charges to watch out for

When applying for a credit card, it's important to understand the fees and charges associated with the card. These fees and charges can include annual fees, interest rates, balance transfer fees, cash advance fees, foreign transaction fees, and late payment fees.

Annual fees are a charge that is typically assessed on a yearly basis for having and using a credit card. Some credit cards do not have an annual fee, while others can have fees that range from a few dollars to hundreds of dollars per year. It's important to understand the annual fee and consider if the benefits and rewards offered by the card outweigh the annual fee.

Interest rates are the charges that are assessed on the unpaid balance of a credit card. The interest rate can vary depending on the type of card and the creditworthiness of the cardholder. It's important to understand the interest rate and consider if the rewards and benefits offered by the card outweigh the interest rate.

Balance transfer fees are charges that are assessed when transferring a balance from one credit card to another. These fees can vary depending on the credit card and the amount of the balance transfer. Some credit cards may offer a promotional rate for balance transfers, but it's important to understand the terms and conditions of the promotion and consider if the long-term interest rate is higher than the promotional rate.

Cash advance fees are charges that are assessed when taking a cash advance from a credit card. These fees can vary depending on the credit card and the amount of the cash advance. Cash advances often have a higher interest rate than purchases made with the card, so it's important to understand the fees and interest rate associated with cash advances and consider if they outweigh the benefits.

How to avoid or minimize credit card fees

When using a credit card, it's important to understand the fees and charges associated with the card and take steps to avoid or minimize them.

One way to avoid or minimize credit card fees is to choose a credit card with no annual fee. Many credit cards offer no annual fee, and some even offer rewards and benefits. By choosing a card with no annual fee, you can save money on a yearly basis and still have access to credit.

Another way to avoid or minimize credit card fees is to pay your balance in full each month. By paying your balance in full, you can avoid interest charges, which can add up quickly and significantly increase the cost of credit. Additionally, by paying your balance in full, you can avoid late payment fees, which are charged when a payment is not received by the due date.

Another way to avoid or minimize credit card fees is to use a credit card with a low interest rate. By using a credit card with a low interest rate, you can reduce the cost of credit and save money over time.

Another way to avoid or minimize credit card fees is to be aware of the fees and charges associated with the card and avoid activities that trigger them. For example, if a card has a high balance transfer fee, it's best to avoid making balance transfers. If a card has a high foreign transaction fee, it's best to use another card when traveling abroad.

Another way to avoid or minimize credit card fees is to use a credit card that offers rewards or cashback. Many credit cards offer rewards or cashback for purchases made with the card. By using a card that offers rewards or cashback, you can offset the cost of the fees and charges associated with the card.

Another way to avoid or minimize credit card fees is to negotiate with your credit card issuer. Sometimes, credit card issuers are willing to waive or reduce fees for customers who have a good history of on-time payments and low balances.

In conclusion, credit card fees can add up quickly and significantly increase the cost of credit. To avoid or minimize credit card fees, choose a credit card with no annual fee, pay your balance in full each month, use a credit card with a low interest rate, be aware of the fees and charges associated with the card, use a credit card that offers rewards or cashback and negotiate with your credit card issuer. By following these tips, you can save money on credit card fees and enjoy the benefits of credit without incurring unnecessary costs.

How to read and understand your credit card statement

Understanding your credit card statement is an important part of managing your credit and ensuring that you are not overcharged or subject to errors on your account. Your credit card statement is a summary of all the transactions you made during a billing cycle, including purchases, cash advances, balance transfers, and payments.

The first thing you should do when you receive your credit card statement is to check the balance. This will give you an idea of how much you owe and when the payment is due. It's important to pay your balance in full by the due date to avoid interest charges and late fees.

Next, you should check for any errors or unauthorized transactions on your statement. Look for any transactions that you do not recognize or that were made without your authorization. If you find any errors or unauthorized transactions, contact your credit card issuer immediately to report the problem and dispute the charges.

You should also check the interest rate and fees charged during the billing cycle. Look for the annual percentage rate (APR) which is the interest rate charged on the unpaid balance, cash advance APR, balance transfer APR, late payment fee, and other charges. Knowing the interest rate and fees associated with your card can help you to make informed decisions about how to use your credit.

Additionally, check the rewards or cashback earned during the billing cycle. If you're using a rewards credit card, look for the rewards earned during the billing cycle and how you can redeem them.

It's also important to check the minimum payment amount due. The minimum payment is the smallest amount that you can pay to keep your account in good standing. Paying the minimum payment can help you avoid late fees, but it's important to remember that it will not pay off your balance in full.

It's important to keep track of your statement and compare it with your records of spending. This will help you to identify any discrepancies or errors, and ensure that you are not being overcharged. It's also a good idea to keep your statements for at least a year, in case you need to refer to them later.

In conclusion, understanding your credit card statement is an important part of managing your credit and ensuring that you are not overcharged or subject to errors on your account. You should check the balance, look for errors or unauthorized transactions, check the interest rate and fees charged during the billing cycle, check the rewards or cashback earned, and the minimum payment amount due. Keep track of your statement, compare it with your records of spending and keep your statements for at least a year, in case you need to refer to them later. By understanding and managing your credit card statement, you can make informed decisions about your credit and avoid unnecessary fees and charges.

CHAPTER FIVE

The Smart Way to Use Credit Cards

How to set a budget and stick to it when using your credit card

Setting a budget and sticking to it when using a credit card is an important step in managing your credit and avoiding overspending. A budget is a plan that helps you to keep track of your income and expenses and ensure that you are living within your means.

The first step in setting a budget is to determine your income. This includes your salary, any bonuses, or other forms of income that you receive. Once you know your income, you can start to create a budget.

Next, you should create a list of all your expenses. This includes your fixed expenses, such as rent or mortgage, utilities, and insurance, as well as your variable expenses, such as food, transportation, and entertainment. It's important to be as detailed as possible when creating your list of expenses, to ensure that you have a realistic budget.

Once you have your income and expenses, you can start to create your budget. The goal is to make sure that your expenses do not exceed your income. If they do, you may need to make adjustments to your expenses, such as cutting back on discretionary spending or increasing your income.

When creating your budget, it's also important to set aside money for unexpected expenses and emergencies. This can help to ensure that you have the funds you need to cover unexpected expenses without having to rely on credit.

When using your credit card, it's important to stick to your budget. This means only using your credit card for purchases that you can afford to pay for with cash. It's also important to pay your credit card balance in full each month to avoid interest charges.

Another important step to stick to your budget is to track your spending. This means keeping track of all your purchases and comparing them to your budget. This will help you to identify areas where you may be overspending, and make adjustments as needed.

Additionally, it's important to set a credit limit for yourself. This means setting a limit on how much you can spend on your credit card each month. This can help to ensure that you do not overspend and get into debt.

In conclusion, setting a budget and sticking to it when using a credit card is an important step in managing your credit and avoiding overspending. The first step is to determine your income, create a list of all your expenses, and create a budget that ensures that your expenses do not exceed your income. When using your credit card, it's important to stick to your budget, pay your credit card balance in full each month, track your spending and set a credit limit for yourself. By following these tips, you can use your credit card responsibly and stay within your means.

Another important tip for sticking to your budget when using your credit card is to use automatic payments. This means setting up automatic payments for your credit card bill, so that you never miss a payment and incur late fees. It's also a good idea to set up reminders for yourself, such as calendar alerts, to help you keep track of your due dates and payments.

It's also important to review your credit card statements regularly. This will help you to stay on top of your spending, identify any errors or unauthorized charges, and ensure that you are not overcharged or subject to interest charges. By reviewing your statements regularly, you can also identify patterns in your spending and make adjustments as needed.

Another way to stick to your budget when using a credit card is to use credit card rewards to your advantage. Many credit cards offer rewards or cashback for purchases made with the card. By using a card that offers rewards or cashback, you can offset the cost of the fees and charges associated with the card.

Lastly, it's important to be mindful of your credit utilization ratio. This is the ratio of the amount of credit you have used to the amount of credit available to you. A high credit utilization ratio can indicate to lenders that you are overusing your credit and may be a risk for default. To avoid this, it's important to keep your credit utilization ratio below 30%.

In conclusion, setting a budget and sticking to it when using a credit card is an important step in managing your credit and avoiding overspending. It's important to stick to your budget, pay your credit card balance in full each month, track your spending, set a credit limit for yourself, use automatic payments, review your credit card statements regularly, use credit card rewards to your advantage and be mindful of your credit utilization ratio. By following these tips, you can use your credit card responsibly and stay within your means.

How to avoid overspending and racking up credit card debt

Overspending and racking up credit card debt can be a major problem for many people. Credit card debt can lead to financial stress, damage to your credit score, and difficulty in meeting your financial goals. To avoid overspending and racking up credit card debt, it's important to have a plan in place and be mindful of your spending habits.

The first step to avoid overspending and racking up credit card debt is to set a budget. A budget is a plan that helps you to keep track of your income and expenses and ensure that you are living within your means. By setting a budget, you can better understand where your money is going and make adjustments as needed.

Another important step to avoid overspending and racking up credit card debt is to track your spending. This means keeping track of all your purchases and comparing them to your budget. This will help you to identify areas where you may be overspending, and make adjustments as needed. Tracking your spending can also help you to identify patterns in your spending and make adjustments as needed.

It's also important to set a credit limit for yourself. This means setting a limit on how much you can spend on your credit card each month. This can help to ensure that you do not overspend and get into debt.

When using your credit card, it's important to pay your balance in full each month. Paying your balance in full helps you to avoid interest charges and late fees, which can add up quickly and significantly increase the cost of credit.

Another way to avoid overspending and racking up credit card debt is to use cash instead of credit. Using cash can help you to better understand the value of money and can make it more difficult to overspend.

It's also important to be mindful of your credit utilization ratio. This is the ratio of the amount of credit you have used to the amount of credit available to you. A high credit utilization ratio can indicate to lenders that you are overusing your credit and may be a risk for default. To avoid this, it's important to keep your credit utilization ratio below 30%.

Another way to avoid overspending and racking up credit card debt is to use credit card rewards to your advantage. Many credit cards offer rewards or cashback for purchases made with the card. By using a card that offers rewards or cashback, you can offset the cost of the fees and charges associated with the card.

Lastly, it's important to be aware of your emotions and mindset when using credit cards. Many people tend to overspend when they are feeling stressed or emotional, so it's important to be aware of your emotions and try to avoid impulse buying.

How to build and maintain a good credit history

Building and maintaining a good credit history is essential for achieving financial goals such as buying a house, car or even getting a personal loan. A good credit history can also help you get approved for credit cards with favorable terms and lower interest rates. Here are some tips on how to build and maintain a good credit history.

The first step in building a good credit history is to get a credit card. Having a credit card and using it responsibly is one of the most effective ways to establish a credit history. It's important to choose a credit card that is right for you and your spending habits.

Once you have a credit card, it's important to use it responsibly. This means making your payments on time and keeping your credit utilization ratio below 30%. Late payments and high credit utilization can have a negative impact on your credit score.

Another important step in building and maintaining a good credit history is to check your credit report regularly. This will help you to identify any errors or inaccuracies that may be hurting your credit score. You can get a free credit report from the three credit bureaus once a year.

It's also important to diversify your credit. This means having a mix of different types of credit accounts, such as credit cards, a personal loan, or a car loan. This shows lenders that you can handle different types of credit responsibly.

Additionally, it's important to maintain a long credit history. The longer your credit history, the better your credit score is likely to be. So, it's important to keep old credit accounts open, even if you are not using them.

Another way to build and maintain a good credit history is to use credit responsibly. This means avoiding applying for too much credit at once, keeping your credit utilization low and avoiding closing accounts too quickly.

Lastly, it's important to avoid bad credit habits such as missing payments, maxing out your credit cards, or falling behind on your bills. These can have a negative impact on your credit score and make it harder to build and maintain a good credit history.

In conclusion, building and maintaining a good credit history is essential for achieving financial goals such as buying a house, car or even getting a personal loan.

CREDIT CARD DEBT DEMOLITION: PROVEN STRATEGIES FOR PAYING IT OFF

Strategies for paying down credit card debt

Paying down credit card debt can be a daunting task, but with the right strategies, it is possible to become debt-free. The first step in paying down credit card debt is to take a close look at your finances and understand how much debt you have and what your options are.

One strategy for paying down credit card debt is to create a budget. A budget can help you to better understand your income and expenses and make adjustments as needed to free up more money to pay down your debt. When creating a budget, it's important to include a line item for debt repayment.

Another strategy for paying down credit card debt is to focus on paying off the card with the highest interest rate first. This is known as the debt snowball method. By focusing on the card with the highest interest rate, you can save money on interest charges and pay off your debt faster.

Another strategy for paying down credit card debt is to transfer your balance to a card with a lower interest rate. This is known as a balance transfer. A balance transfer can help you to save money on interest charges and pay off your debt faster.

Another strategy for paying down credit card debt is to consider a debt consolidation loan. A debt consolidation loan can help you to combine multiple credit card balances into one loan, with a lower interest rate.

Another strategy for paying down credit card debt is to negotiate with your creditors. This can include asking for a lower interest rate or a payment plan. It's important to remember that creditors want to get paid and may be willing to work with you to help you pay off your debt.

Another strategy for paying down credit card debt is to increase your income. This can include getting a part-time job, selling items you no longer need, or renting out a room in your home.

Lastly, it's important to avoid overusing credit cards while paying off your debt. This means avoiding adding to your debt by using credit cards for new purchases. It's also important to avoid opening new credit accounts while paying off your debt.

In conclusion, paying down credit card debt can be a daunting task, but with the right strategies, it is possible to become debt-free. Strategies include creating a budget, focusing on paying off the card with the highest interest rate first, transferring your balance to a card with a lower interest rate, considering a debt consolidation loan, negotiating with creditors, increasing your income and avoiding overusing credit cards while paying off your debt. By following these strategies, you can develop a plan to pay down your credit card debt and become debt-free.

How to negotiate with your credit card issuer to reduce or eliminate fees or interest

Negotiating with your credit card issuer to reduce or eliminate fees or interest can be a powerful tool in managing your credit card debt and improving your financial situation. Credit card issuers want to keep their customers happy and may be willing to work with you to reduce or eliminate fees or interest if you approach them in the right way.

The first step in negotiating with your credit card issuer is to gather information about your account. This includes your account balance, payment history, and any fees or interest charges that you have incurred. Having this information will help you to make a strong case for reducing or eliminating fees or interest.

Next, you should contact your credit card issuer. This can be done by phone or in writing. When you contact your credit card issuer, it's important to be polite and professional. Explain your situation and the reason why you are requesting a reduction or elimination of fees or interest.

When negotiating with your credit card issuer, it's important to have a specific request in mind. For example, you may request a lower interest rate, a waiver of a late fee, or a reduction in an annual fee.

It's also a good idea to be prepared to offer something in return for the reduction or elimination of fees or interest. This can include a promise to pay off your balance in full, to make a lump sum payment, or to make automatic payments.

Another important strategy when negotiating with your credit card issuer is to be persistent. If your request is denied, you can try again at a later date. It's also a good idea to follow up with the credit card issuer to ensure that the agreement has been implemented.

It's also important to be aware of your rights as a consumer. You can check the Fair Credit Billing Act (FCBA) and the Credit CARD Act of 2009, both of which provide protection for credit card holders.

Additionally, it's important to consider other options if the negotiation is not successful. This can include looking for a credit card with lower interest rates or fees, transferring the balance to a lower interest rate card, or considering debt consolidation.

Another tip when negotiating with your credit card issuer is to be willing to walk away. If your credit card issuer is unwilling to negotiate or to provide you with a satisfactory solution, it may be time to consider other options such as closing the account, or looking for a new credit card with better terms.

It's also important to remember that any agreements made with the credit card issuer should be in writing. This will ensure that the agreement is legally binding and that both parties understand the terms of the agreement.

In conclusion, negotiating with your credit card issuer to reduce or eliminate fees or interest can be a powerful tool in managing your credit card debt and improving your financial situation. It's important to gather information about your account, contact your credit card issuer in a polite and professional manner, have a specific request in mind, be prepared to offer something in return, be persistent and be aware of your rights as a consumer. Additionally, if the negotiation is not successful, consider other options such as closing the account or looking for a new credit card with better terms. Remember to have any agreements made in writing to ensure that the agreement is legally binding and that both parties understand the terms of the agreement.

How to work with a credit counselor or debt management service

Working with a credit counselor or debt management service can be an effective way to manage your credit card debt and improve your financial situation. These organizations provide a range of services, including debt management plans, credit counseling, and financial education.

The first step in working with a credit counselor or debt management service is to choose a reputable organization. It's important to choose an organization that is a member of the National Foundation for Credit Counseling (NFCC) or the Association of Independent Consumer Credit Counseling Agencies (AICCCA). These organizations have strict standards for their members, and they are a good indication of the quality of the service you will receive.

When working with a credit counselor or debt management service, you will typically be asked to provide information about your income, expenses, and debt. The counselor will use this information to create a budget and develop a debt management plan that is tailored to your individual needs.

A debt management plan is a repayment plan that is designed to help you pay off your debt over a period of time. This typically involves consolidating your credit card debt into one monthly payment, and the credit counselor will negotiate with your creditors to lower interest rates and waive fees.

Credit counseling involves working with a counselor to understand your financial situation and develop a plan to improve it. This may include budgeting, saving, and investing advice as well as credit report review and credit score improvement strategies.

Financial education is another important aspect of working with a credit counselor or debt management service. This includes learning about budgeting, saving, and investing, as well as understanding credit reports, credit scores and how credit card interest and fees work.

It's important to remember that working with a credit counselor or debt management service is a commitment and it may take time to see results. It's important to be patient and stay committed to the plan.

When working with a credit counselor or debt management service, it's important to be honest and upfront about your financial situation. This will help the counselor to develop a plan that is tailored to your needs and that you can realistically follow.

It's also important to be aware of the fees associated with working with a credit counselor or debt management service. Some organizations may charge fees for their services, while others may be non-profit and offer services for free.

In conclusion, working with a credit counselor or debt management service can be an effective way to manage your credit card debt and improve your financial situation. It's important to choose a reputable organization, be honest and upfront about your financial situation, be patient and committed to the plan, and be aware of any fees associated with the service. By working with a credit counselor or debt management service, you can develop a plan to pay off your debt and improve your financial situation.

CHAPTER SEVEN

HOW TO DISPUTE A CHARGE ON YOUR CREDIT CARD

What to do if you spot an unauthorized charge on your credit card statement

If you spot an unauthorized charge on your credit card statement, it's important to take immediate action to protect yourself from further fraud. The first step is to contact your credit card issuer as soon as possible. Most credit card issuers have a toll-free number that you can call to report the unauthorized charge. It's important to have your credit card statement handy so that you can provide the credit card issuer with the necessary information, such as the date of the charge, the amount of the charge, and the merchant name.

When you report the unauthorized charge, the credit card issuer will typically place a temporary credit on your account for the amount of the charge. This means that the charge will be removed from your account and you will not be responsible for paying it.

Your credit card issuer will then start an investigation into the unauthorized charge. They will contact the merchant where the charge was made and ask for more information. This process can take several weeks to complete, and you will be informed of the outcome.

While the investigation is ongoing, it's important to keep an eye on your credit card statement and report any additional unauthorized charges that you spot.

It's also important to take steps to protect your credit card information in order to prevent further unauthorized charges. You can do this by keeping an eye on your credit card statement to make sure that all the charges are legitimate, and by reviewing your credit report to ensure that there are no suspicious accounts or charges.

Additionally, it's important to be aware of the Fair Credit Billing Act (FCBA) which provides protection for credit card holders in case of billing errors or unauthorized charges. Under the FCBA, if you report an unauthorized charge within 60 days of the statement on which the unauthorized charge first appeared, you are only liable for up to $50 of the unauthorized charge.

Another important step to take is to consider freezing or locking your credit to prevent any new accounts from being opened in your name.

In conclusion, if you spot an unauthorized charge on your credit card statement, it's important to take immediate action to protect yourself from further fraud. Report the unauthorized charge to your credit card issuer as soon as possible, keep an eye on your credit card statement, review your credit report, be aware of the FCBA, and consider freezing or locking your credit. By taking these steps, you can protect yourself from further fraud and ensure that the unauthorized charge is resolved quickly.

How to file a dispute with your credit card issuer

Filing a dispute with your credit card issuer is an important step to take if you believe there is an error on your statement or if you spot an unauthorized charge. The process of filing a dispute can vary depending on your credit card issuer, but there are some general steps that you can follow to ensure that your dispute is handled quickly and effectively.

The first step in filing a dispute is to gather the necessary documentation. This includes your credit card statement, receipts, and any other documentation that supports your dispute. This information will be used by the credit card issuer to investigate the dispute.

The next step is to contact your credit card issuer. Most credit card issuers have a toll-free number that you can call to report the dispute. You can also file a dispute online or by mail. When you contact your credit card issuer, it's important to be polite and professional and have all the necessary documentation ready.

When you file a dispute, the credit card issuer will typically place a temporary credit on your account for the disputed amount. This means that the disputed charge will be removed from your account and you will not be responsible for paying it until the dispute is resolved.

The credit card issuer will then start an investigation into the dispute. This process can take several weeks to complete, and you will be informed of the outcome. During the investigation, it's important to keep an eye on your credit card statement and report any additional disputed charges that you spot.

It's also important to be aware of the Fair Credit Billing Act (FCBA) which provides protection for credit card holders in case of billing errors or unauthorized charges. Under the FCBA, if you report a dispute within 60 days of the statement on which the disputed charge first appeared, you are not liable for the disputed charge while the dispute is being investigated.

It's also important to make note of any deadlines set by your credit card issuer for filing disputes and follow up on the status of your dispute. If you are not satisfied with the outcome, you have the right to appeal and can reach out to the Consumer Financial Protection Bureau (CFPB) for assistance.

In conclusion, filing a dispute with your credit card issuer is an important step to take if you believe there is an error on your statement or if you spot an unauthorized charge. Gather the necessary documentation, contact your credit card issuer, be aware of the FCBA, and keep an eye on your credit card statement during the investigation. Additionally, make note of any deadlines set by your credit card issuer for filing disputes, follow up on the status of your dispute and if needed, reach out to the CFPB for assistance. By following these steps, you can ensure that your dispute is handled quickly and effectively.

What to expect during the dispute resolution process

The dispute resolution process is the process of resolving a dispute between a credit card holder and the credit card issuer. The process can vary depending on the credit card issuer, but there are some general steps that you can expect to experience during the process.

The first step in the dispute resolution process is to file a dispute with your credit card issuer. This can be done by contacting your credit card issuer, either by phone, online or by mail. When you file a dispute, it's important to provide the credit card issuer with all the necessary documentation that supports your dispute, such as receipts, invoices, and any other relevant information.

Once the dispute has been filed, the credit card issuer will typically place a temporary credit on your account for the disputed amount. This means that the disputed charge will be removed from your account, and you will not be responsible for paying it until the dispute is resolved.

The next step in the process is the investigation. The credit card issuer will investigate the dispute and will contact the merchant where the charge was made and ask for more information. This process can take several weeks to complete, and you will be informed of the outcome.

During the investigation, it's important to keep an eye on your credit card statement and report any additional disputed charges that you spot. This will ensure that the credit card issuer is aware of all disputed charges, and the investigation can be completed as quickly as possible.

Once the investigation is complete, the credit card issuer will make a decision on the dispute. If the dispute is found in your favor, the disputed charge will be removed from your account and you will not be responsible for paying it. If the dispute is not found in your favor, the disputed charge will be added back to your account, and you will be responsible for paying it.

It's also important to be aware of the Fair Credit Billing Act (FCBA) which provides protection for credit card holders in case of billing errors or unauthorized charges. Under the FCBA, if you report a dispute within 60 days of the statement on which the disputed charge first appeared, you are not liable for the disputed charge while the dispute is being investigated.

In addition, it's important to follow up on the status of your dispute and make note of any deadlines set by your credit card issuer for filing disputes. If you are not satisfied with the outcome, you have the right to appeal, and can reach out to the Consumer Financial Protection Bureau (CFPB) for assistance.

In conclusion, during the dispute resolution process, you can expect to file a dispute, have a temporary credit applied to your account, have your dispute investigated, receive a decision on the dispute, be aware of the FCBA, follow up on the status of your dispute, make note of any deadlines set by your credit card issuer for filing disputes and if needed, reach out to the CFPB for assistance. By understanding the process and being prepared for what to expect, you can navigate the dispute resolution process with confidence and ensure that your dispute is handled quickly and effectively. It's also important to remember that the dispute resolution process can be time-consuming, and it may take several weeks or even months to resolve. It's important to be patient and persistent throughout the process, and to keep all your documentation and records organized and up-to-date.

During the process, it's also important to be aware of the possible outcomes of the dispute, such as having the disputed charge removed from your account, having the disputed charge added back to your account, or having the dispute resolved in a different manner. Depending on the outcome, it may be necessary to take additional steps to protect your credit history, such as disputing the charge with the merchant directly or filing a complaint with the Consumer Financial Protection Bureau (CFPB) if you believe that your rights under the Fair Credit Billing Act (FCBA) have been violated.

It's also important to keep in mind that credit card disputes can have an impact on your credit score, so it's important to take a measured and thoughtful approach to the process and to consider the potential consequences of your actions.

In summary, the dispute resolution process can be a complex and time-consuming process, but by understanding what to expect, gathering necessary documentation, being aware of your rights under the FCBA, following up on the status of your dispute, and seeking help if needed, you can navigate the process successfully and resolve your dispute in a timely manner.

CHAPTER EIGHT

Fraud Prevention Pro: Mastering the Art of Credit Card Security

How to spot and report credit card fraud

Credit card fraud is a serious issue that can have a major impact on your financial well-being. It's important to be vigilant and aware of the signs of credit card fraud so that you can take immediate action to protect yourself.

One of the most common signs of credit card fraud is the presence of unauthorized charges on your credit card statement. If you spot charges that you don't recognize, it's important to investigate them immediately. You should also be on the lookout for charges that are made in unusual locations or at odd hours.

Another sign of credit card fraud is the receipt of bills or statements for credit cards or accounts that you didn't open. This can be a sign that someone has stolen your personal information and is using it to open new accounts in your name.

You should also be on the lookout for any suspicious activity on your credit report. If you notice accounts or charges that you don't recognize, it's important to investigate them immediately. This could be a sign that someone has taken out loans or opened credit accounts in your name.

Additionally, you should be on the lookout for any suspicious phone calls, emails, or text messages, claiming to be from your credit card issuer or bank. These scams, often called "phishing" attempts, are designed to trick you into giving away your personal information, such as your credit card number, expiration date, and CVV code.

If you suspect that you're a victim of credit card fraud, it's important to take immediate action to protect yourself. The first step is to contact your credit card issuer as soon as possible. Most credit card issuers have a toll-free number that you can call to report the fraud. You should also report the fraud to the Federal Trade Commission (FTC) and to the three major credit bureaus.

It's also important to take steps to protect your credit card information in order to prevent further fraud. You can do this by keeping an eye on your credit card statement to make sure that all the charges are legitimate, and by reviewing your credit report to ensure that there are no suspicious accounts or charges.

Additionally, consider freezing or locking your credit to prevent any new accounts from being opened in your name.

It's also important to be aware of the Fair Credit Billing Act (FCBA) which provides protection for credit card holders in case of unauthorized charges. Under the FCBA, if you report an unauthorized charge within 60 days of the statement on which the unauthorized charge first appeared, you are only liable for up to $50 of the unauthorized charge.

In conclusion, being aware of the signs of credit card fraud, reporting it to the authorities, protecting your credit information, freezing or locking your credit and being aware of the FCBA are important steps to take to protect yourself from credit card fraud. By taking these steps, you can protect yourself from further fraud and ensure that the unauthorized charge is resolved quickly.

Tips for keeping your credit card information safe online and offline

Keeping your credit card information safe is essential to protect yourself from credit card fraud. Here are some tips that you can follow to keep your credit card information safe both online and offline.

1. Be cautious of phishing scams: Be wary of unsolicited emails, text messages, or phone calls that claim to be from your credit card issuer or bank. These scams, often called "phishing" attempts, are designed to trick you into giving away your personal information, such as your credit card number, expiration date, and CVV code.
2. Use a secure website: When making online purchases, make sure the website is secure by looking for the padlock icon in the browser, and the website starts with "https." This ensures that any information you enter will be encrypted, making it much harder for hackers to steal your information.
3. Use a credit card instead of a debit card: Credit cards offer more protection than debit cards in case of unauthorized charges. Under the Fair Credit Billing Act (FCBA), if you report an unauthorized charge within 60 days of the statement on which the unauthorized charge first appeared, you are only liable for up to $50 of the unauthorized charge.
4. Use a virtual credit card number: Some credit card issuers offer the option of generating a virtual credit card number that can be used for online purchases. This number is different from your actual credit card number and can be used for a single

transaction or a specific time frame, adding an extra layer of
security to your transactions.

5. Keep your credit card in a safe place: When not in use, keep
your credit card in a safe place, such as a locked drawer or
wallet. This will prevent someone from stealing your credit
card and using it to make unauthorized purchases.

6. Keep your credit card information private: Do not share your
credit card information with anyone, and never give it out over
the phone or through an email. It's also important to be aware
of shoulder surfers, who might try to steal your credit card
information by looking over your shoulder while you're
making a purchase.

7. Use a credit card monitoring service: Some credit card issuers
offer credit card monitoring services that will notify you of any
suspicious activity on your credit card. This can be an effective
way to catch fraudulent activity early on and prevent further
damage.

8. Regularly check your credit card statement: Review your credit
card statement regularly to check for any unauthorized
charges. Be sure to report any suspicious activity to your credit
card issuer as soon as possible.

9. Use multi-factor authentication: Multi-factor authentication is
an added layer of security that requires a second form of
identification, such as a fingerprint or a code sent to your
phone, in addition to your password, to access your account.
This makes it much harder for hackers to gain access to your
account.

In conclusion, keeping your credit card information safe is
essential to protect yourself from credit card fraud. By being
cautious of phishing scams, using a secure website, using a credit
card instead of a debit card, using a virtual credit card number,
keeping your credit card in a safe place, keeping your credit card

information private, using a credit card monitoring service, regularly checking your credit card statement and using multi-factor authentication, you can help keep your credit card information safe and secure.

How to recover from credit card fraud

Recovering from credit card fraud can be a difficult and time-consuming process, but there are steps that you can take to minimize the damage and protect yourself going forward.

Report the fraud immediately: The first step in recovering from credit card fraud is to report it as soon as possible to your credit card issuer. Most credit card issuers have a toll-free number that you can call to report the fraud. You should also report the fraud to the Federal Trade Commission (FTC) and to the three major credit bureaus.

Review your credit report: Review your credit report to ensure that there are no suspicious accounts or charges. You can obtain a free copy of your credit report from the three major credit bureaus - TransUnion, Equifax, and Experian - once a year.

Close any compromised accounts: If your credit card has been compromised, it's important to close the account to prevent further fraud. Your credit card issuer should be able to do this for you.

Monitor your credit: It's important to monitor your credit going forward to ensure that no new fraudulent accounts have been opened in your name. You can sign up for a credit monitoring service, or you can monitor your credit report yourself.

Change any associated passwords: If your credit card was used to make purchases online, it's important to change the password associated with that account to prevent further fraud.

Check your bank account and credit card statements regularly: It's important to keep a close eye on your bank account and credit card statements to ensure that there are no unauthorized charges.

File a police report: If you suspect that your credit card information has been stolen, you should file a police report. This will help to document the fraud and can be used as evidence in court if necessary.

Consider freezing or locking your credit: Consider freezing or locking your credit to prevent any new accounts from being opened in your name.

Take steps to prevent future fraud: Take steps to protect yourself from future fraud, such as being cautious of phishing scams, keeping your credit card information private, and using a credit card monitoring service.

Seek professional help if needed: If you are having trouble resolving the fraud or if it has caused financial difficulties, consider reaching out to a credit counselor or a debt management service for help.

Recovering from credit card fraud can be a difficult and time-consuming process, but by following these steps, you can minimize the damage and protect yourself going forward. It's important to stay vigilant and keep a close eye on your credit and financial accounts to ensure that there are no further unauthorized charges. Additionally, it's important to take steps to prevent future fraud, such as being cautious of phishing scams, keeping your credit card information private, and using a credit card monitoring service.

It's also important to keep in mind that credit card fraud can have an impact on your credit score, so it's important to take a measured and thoughtful approach to the process and to consider the potential consequences of your actions.

Additionally, it's important to take steps to prevent future fraud, such as using a credit card with a chip, using a virtual credit card number, and only using trusted and secure websites for online purchases.

In summary, recovering from credit card fraud can be a challenging process, but by taking the necessary steps to report the fraud, reviewing your credit report, closing compromised accounts, monitoring your credit, changing associated passwords, checking your bank account and credit card statements regularly, filing a police report, freezing or locking your credit, taking steps to prevent future fraud and seeking professional help if needed, you can minimize the damage and protect yourself going forward.

The Ultimate Credit Boost: Proven Strategies for Improving Your Score

What goes into your credit score and how to improve it

Your credit score is a numerical value that represents your creditworthiness. It is used by lenders to determine your eligibility for credit and loans, as well as the interest rate you will be charged. A good credit score can make it easier to get approved for credit and loans, and can also result in lower interest rates and other favorable terms.

The most widely used credit score is the FICO score, which is based on information from the three major credit bureaus: TransUnion, Equifax, and Experian. The FICO score ranges from 300 to 850, with a score above 700 considered to be good.

There are several factors that go into determining your FICO score, including:

1. Payment history: This accounts for 35% of your FICO score, and is based on your history of paying bills on time. Late payments can have a negative impact on your score, while a consistent history of on-time payments can help to improve it.
2. Credit utilization: This accounts for 30% of your FICO score, and is based on how much of your available credit you are using. Using a high percentage of your available credit can have a negative impact on your score, while keeping your credit usage low can help to improve it.
3. Length of credit history: This accounts for 15% of your FICO score, and is based on the length of time that you have had credit. A longer credit history can be beneficial for your score, while a shorter history can have a negative impact.

4. Types of credit: This accounts for 10% of your FICO score, and is based on the types of credit that you have. Having a mix of different types of credit, such as a mortgage, car loan, and credit card, can be beneficial for your score.

5. New credit: This accounts for 10% of your FICO score, and is based on how many new credit accounts you have opened recently. Opening too many new accounts in a short period of time can have a negative impact on your score.

6. Here are some tips on how to improve your credit score:

7. Pay your bills on time: Make sure to pay all of your bills on time, as late payments can have a negative impact on your score.

8. Keep your credit utilization low: Try to keep your credit utilization at 30% or less of your total credit limit.

9. Don't close old credit accounts: Keep your old credit accounts open, as they can help to boost the length of your credit history.

10. Limit new credit applications: Avoid applying for new credit too frequently, as it can have a negative impact on your score.

11. Dispute credit report errors: Review your credit report for errors and dispute any inaccuracies with the credit bureau.

12. Keep a mix of credit: Having a mix of different types of credit, such as a mortgage, car loan, and credit card can be beneficial for your score.

13. Use credit cards responsibly: Use your credit cards responsibly by paying off balances in full and on time each month. Avoid maxing out your credit cards as it will increase your credit utilization and negatively impact your score.

14. Consider a secured credit card: If you have a limited credit history or a poor credit score, consider getting a secured credit card. This type of credit card requires a deposit, which becomes the credit limit, making it easier to be approved and it can help you to rebuild your credit.

15. Seek professional help if needed: If you're struggling to improve your credit score or you're overwhelmed by credit card debt, consider reaching out to a credit counselor or a debt management service for help.

Remember, improving your credit score takes time and effort, it is not a quick fix. It is important to be patient and consistent in your efforts to improve your score. With a good credit score, you'll have more options for credit and loans, and you'll be able to take advantage of the best terms and interest rates. It's worth it to take the time to understand your credit score and take steps to improve it.

How to check your credit report and dispute errors

Checking your credit report is an important step in understanding your creditworthiness and identifying any errors that may be affecting your credit score. The Fair Credit Reporting Act (FCRA) requires the three major credit bureaus - TransUnion, Equifax, and Experian - to provide you with a free copy of your credit report once a year. You can request your report online at annualcreditreport.com or by calling 1-877-322-8228.

When you receive your credit report, it's important to review it carefully for errors. Some common errors to look for include:

1. Incorrect personal information: Make sure that your name, address, and other personal information are correct.
2. Inaccurate credit accounts: Make sure that all of the credit accounts listed on your report are accurate and belong to you.
3. Inaccurate payment history: Check that your payment history is accurate and that all late payments are correctly reflected.
4. Inaccurate credit limit: Check that the credit limit on each account is correct.
5. Duplicate accounts: Make sure that there are no duplicate accounts listed.
6. Inaccurate public records: Check that any public records listed on your report are accurate, including bankruptcies and foreclosures.

If you find errors on your credit report, you can dispute them with the credit bureau that issued the report. Here's how to dispute errors on your credit report:

1. Gather evidence: Collect any documentation that supports your dispute, such as bank statements, receipts, or letters from the creditor.
2. Write a dispute letter: Write a letter to the credit bureau disputing the errors on your report. Be sure to include your personal information, the errors you are disputing, and any supporting documentation.
3. Submit your dispute: Submit your dispute letter to the credit bureau by mail or online. Be sure to include copies of any supporting documentation.
4. Wait for a response: The credit bureau has 30 days to investigate your dispute and respond to you.
5. Follow up: If the credit bureau doesn't respond or doesn't resolve the errors to your satisfaction, you can follow up with them.

It's also important to note that if the credit bureau finds that the disputed information is inaccurate, they must notify the creditor or the information provider of the dispute and provide them with a copy of your dispute letter. The creditor or the information provider then has to investigate, review the relevant information and report the results back to the credit bureau.

It's important to check your credit report regularly for errors, as even small mistakes can have a big impact on your credit score. Dispute any errors you find with the credit bureau and follow up to make sure that the errors are corrected. This can help to improve your credit score and ensure that your credit report accurately reflects your creditworthiness.

How to rebuild your credit after a financial setback

Rebuilding your credit after a financial setback can be a challenging task, but it's not impossible. A financial setback can come in many forms, such as a job loss, medical emergency, divorce, or even a mistake such as missing a credit card payment. Whatever the cause, the important thing is to take action to start rebuilding your credit as soon as possible. Here are some steps you can take to rebuild your credit:

1. Review your credit report: Before you can start rebuilding your credit, you need to know where you stand. Obtain a copy of your credit report from each of the three major credit bureaus and review it for errors. Dispute any errors you find with the credit bureau and follow up to make sure that the errors are corrected.
2. Make a budget: Take a good look at your income and expenses and create a budget that allows you to pay all your bills on time. This will be the foundation for rebuilding your credit.
3. Prioritize paying off debt: High levels of debt can have a negative impact on your credit score. Prioritize paying off the debt with the highest interest rate first.
4. Keep your credit utilization low: Your credit utilization, which is the amount of credit you're using compared to the amount of credit available to you, accounts for 30% of your credit score. Try to keep your credit utilization at 30% or lower.
5. Make payments on time: Late payments can have a negative impact on your credit score. If you're having trouble making payments on time, reach out to your creditors and explain your situation. They may be able to work with you to develop a

payment plan.

6. Consider a secured credit card: If you have a limited credit history or a poor credit score, consider getting a secured credit card. This type of credit card requires a deposit, which becomes the credit limit, making it easier to be approved and it can help you to rebuild your credit.
7. Be patient: Rebuilding your credit takes time and effort. It's important to be patient and consistent in your efforts.
8. Seek professional help if needed: If you're struggling to rebuild your credit or you're overwhelmed by debt, consider reaching out to a credit counselor or a debt management service for help.

It's important to remember that rebuilding your credit after a financial setback is a process that takes time and effort. It's important to be patient and consistent in your efforts. By taking the steps outlined above, you can take control of your finances and start rebuilding your credit.

CHAPTER TEN

Clearing the Credit Haze: Answering Common Questions on Indian Credit Cards

Can you have more than one credit card in India?'.

In India, it is possible to have more than one credit card. There is no legal limit on the number of credit cards one can have. However, having multiple credit cards can come with its own set of challenges and responsibilities.

There are several benefits to having multiple credit cards:

Credit diversity: Having a mix of credit cards from different issuers can help to diversify your credit mix, which can be beneficial for your credit score.

Rewards and benefits: Different credit cards offer different rewards and benefits, such as cashback, reward points, or travel miles. Having multiple credit cards can allow you to take advantage of these different rewards and benefits.

Emergency funds: Having multiple credit cards can provide you with a backup source of funds in case of an emergency.

However, having multiple credit cards also comes with its own set of responsibilities:

Managing multiple payments: You will need to keep track of multiple credit card balances and payments, which can be challenging.

Higher credit utilization: Having multiple credit cards can lead to higher credit utilization, which can negatively impact your credit score.

Increased risk of overspending: Having multiple credit cards can increase the temptation to overspend, which can lead to credit card debt.

Higher fees and interest rates: Some credit cards come with higher fees and interest rates, which can add up over time.

If you're considering getting another credit card, it's important to evaluate your current financial situation and your ability to manage multiple credit card accounts responsibly. It is also important to compare and choose credit cards that are best suited for your needs. Also, make sure to keep track of your credit utilization, as it is one of the most important factors in determining your credit score and it is advisable to keep it below 30%. Also, make sure to make all credit card payments on time, as late payments can lead to late payment fees and negatively impact your credit score.

Before applying for another credit card, It is advisable to review your current credit score and credit history, as well as your income and expenses, to ensure that you can manage another credit card responsibly.

How to report a lost or stolen credit card in India?

Losing a credit card or having it stolen can be a stressful and frustrating experience, but it's important to act quickly to minimize the potential damage. Here are the steps you need to take to report a lost or stolen credit card in India:

1. Call your credit card issuer: As soon as you realize that your credit card is lost or stolen, call your credit card issuer to report the loss. Most credit card issuers have a 24-hour customer service hotline that you can call.
2. Provide your account information: When you call your credit card issuer, you'll be asked to provide your account information, such as your card number, expiration date, and security code.
3. Request that your card be blocked or canceled: Once you've reported the loss, your credit card issuer will block or cancel your card to prevent unauthorized use.
4. Request a replacement card: After your card has been blocked or canceled, you can request a replacement card.
5. File a police complaint: You should also file a police complaint regarding the loss or theft of the credit card. This will help you in case of any fraud.
6. Keep records: Keep a record of all the conversation you made with the credit card issuer and the police, along with the complaint number.
7. Check your account statement: After you report the loss, monitor your account statement closely to ensure that no unauthorized charges have been made.

8. Notify the bank of any unauthorized charges: If you find any unauthorized charges on your account, notify your credit card issuer immediately. They will investigate the charges and, if they are found to be fraudulent, they will be removed from your account.

It's important to note that you are generally not liable for unauthorized charges made on a lost or stolen credit card, as per the provisions of the Credit Card Act 2006. However, you should still report the loss as soon as possible to minimize the risk of fraudulent activity.

In conclusion, reporting a lost or stolen credit card in India requires quick action on your part to minimize the potential damage. It's important to call your credit card issuer as soon as possible to report the loss, request that your card be blocked or canceled, and request a replacement card. Also, File a police complaint and keep records of all the conversation you made with the credit card issuer and the police, along with the complaint number. Finally, monitor your account statement closely to ensure that no unauthorized charges have been made, and notify the bank of any unauthorized charges.

How to close a credit card account in India?

Closing a credit card account in India can be a straightforward process, but there are certain steps that you need to take to ensure that the process goes smoothly. Here are the steps you need to take to close a credit card account in India:

1. Pay off any outstanding balance: Before you close your credit card account, make sure that you pay off any outstanding balance. Closing a credit card account with an outstanding balance can have a negative impact on your credit score.
2. Check for any annual or other fees: Some credit cards may have annual or other fees that need to be paid before you can close the account. Make sure to check for any such fees and pay them before closing the account.
3. Contact customer service: Contact your credit card issuer's customer service department to request that the account be closed. You can do this through phone, email, or online chat.
4. Provide your account information: When you contact customer service, you'll be asked to provide your account information, such as your card number and expiration date.
5. Confirm the account closure: Once you've requested that the account be closed, your credit card issuer will confirm the account closure.
6. Cut up the card: Once you receive confirmation that the account has been closed, cut up the card to prevent any future use.
7. Check your credit report: After the account has been closed, check your credit report to ensure that the account has been closed and that the balance is zero.

8. Consider the impact on your credit score: Closing a credit card account can have an impact on your credit score, especially if you have a long credit history with that card or if it's one of your oldest accounts. It's important to consider this before closing an account.

When you decide to close a credit card account, it's important to consider the impact it might have on your credit score, as well as any outstanding balance and annual or other fees. Close the account only if you are sure that it will be beneficial for you.

In conclusion, closing a credit card account in India requires paying off any outstanding balance, checking for any annual or other fees, contacting customer service, providing your account information, confirm the account closure, cutting up the card, checking your credit report, and considering the impact on your credit score. It's important to take these steps to ensure that the process goes smoothly and that the account is closed correctly.

How to check credit card balance and transaction history in India?

Checking your credit card balance and transaction history in India is a crucial step in managing your credit card responsibly. Here are the ways to check your credit card balance and transaction history in India:

1. Online banking: Most credit card issuers in India offer online banking services where you can log in to your account and check your balance and transaction history.
2. Mobile banking: Many credit card issuers also offer mobile banking apps where you can check your balance and transaction history on the go.
3. SMS or email alerts: Some credit card issuers offer SMS or email alerts to notify you of your current balance, payment due dates, and recent transactions.
4. Phone banking: You can also check your credit card balance and transaction history by calling your credit card issuer's phone banking service.
5. Credit card statement: You can check your credit card balance and transaction history by reviewing your monthly statement. This will usually be sent to you via mail or email.
6. Credit report: You can also check your credit card balance and transaction history by reviewing your credit report. It's important to check your credit report regularly to ensure that the information is accurate and to spot any fraudulent activity.
7. Automatic Teller Machine (ATM): You can check your credit card balance and recent transactions by using the ATM.

It's important to regularly check your credit card balance and transaction history to ensure that you are aware of your current balance, recent transactions, and to spot any potential fraudulent activity. By doing this, you can manage your credit card responsibly and make sure that you make timely payments to avoid late fees and interest charges.

In conclusion, checking your credit card balance and transaction history in India can be done through online banking, mobile banking, SMS or email alerts, phone banking, credit card statement, credit report, and Automatic Teller Machine (ATM). It's important to regularly check your balance and transaction history to manage your credit card responsibly, make timely payments, avoid late fees and interest charges, and to spot any potential fraudulent activity.

What happens when you don't pay credit card bill in India?

Not paying your credit card bill in India can have serious consequences that can damage your credit score and financial well-being. Here are the potential consequences of not paying your credit card bill in India:

1. Late fees: If you don't pay your credit card bill on time, you'll be charged a late fee. The late fee can vary depending on the credit card issuer and the amount of the bill.
2. Interest charges: If you don't pay your credit card bill on time, you'll also be charged interest on the outstanding balance. The interest rate can vary depending on the credit card issuer and the amount of the bill.
3. Credit score: Not paying your credit card bill on time can negatively impact your credit score. Late payments are reported to the credit bureaus, and a history of late payments can lower your credit score.
4. Credit limit reduction: Not paying your credit card bill on time can lead to a reduction of your credit limit, which can make it harder to make large purchases in the future.
5. Legal action: If you don't pay your credit card bill for an extended period of time, your credit card issuer may take legal action to collect the debt.
6. Harassment: Credit card issuer may contact you through phone, email, or mail to remind you to pay your bill and may also use the services of collection agencies, which can be harassing.
7. Loss of access to credit: If you have a history of not paying your credit card bill on time, it may be harder for you to get

approved for credit in the future.

8. Credit counseling: If you're having trouble paying your credit card bill, you may want to consider credit counseling. A credit counselor can help you create a budget and a plan to pay off your debt.

It's important to note that it is always best to pay your credit card bill on time to avoid any of the above consequences. If you're struggling to pay your credit card bill, it's best to reach out to your credit card issuer and try to work out a payment plan.

In conclusion, not paying your credit card bill in India can have serious consequences such as late fees, interest charges, credit score, credit limit reduction, legal action, harassment, loss of access to credit, and credit counseling. It's best to pay your credit card bill on time and if you're struggling to pay it reach out to your credit card issuer and try to work out a payment plan. It's important to be aware of the potential consequences of not paying your credit card bill to avoid damaging your credit score and financial well-being.

Conclusion

In conclusion, this guide has provided a comprehensive overview of using credit cards in India. It has covered a wide range of topics including the benefits and drawbacks of using a credit card, how credit cards differ from other forms of credit, how to apply for a credit card, how to compare and choose a credit card, tips for using credit cards responsibly, and how to manage and pay off credit card debt. It also covered topics such as how to dispute a charge on your credit card, how to protect yourself from credit card fraud, and how to improve your credit score. The guide has also provided answers to frequently asked questions about using credit cards in India.

It is important to remember that credit cards can be a powerful financial tool, but they also come with risks and responsibilities. By following the advice in this guide, you can use your credit card to your advantage and avoid the pitfalls that can lead to financial trouble. It's important to always pay your bill on time, keep your balance low, and monitor your account regularly. If you're ever in doubt about something related to your credit card, don't hesitate to reach out to your credit card issuer for clarification.

By understanding the ins and outs of using a credit card, you'll be able to make informed decisions about credit and take control of your financial future.

Last Word

"

Thank you for reading "The Credit Card Bible". We hope that this book has provided you with the information and strategies you need to make about your credit card.

As you turn the last page of this guide, we hope that you've gained a wealth of knowledge on the topic of credit cards in India. From the benefits and drawbacks of using a credit card, to how credit cards differ from other forms of credit, and the documentation and eligibility requirements for applying for a credit card in India, we've covered it all. And let's not forget the valuable tips and strategies on using credit cards responsibly, paying down credit card debt, protecting yourself from credit card fraud and improving your credit score. You are now equipped with the tools to navigate the world of credit cards with confidence and make the most of your credit card while managing it effectively.

As a token of appreciation for taking the time to read this guide, we would like to invite you to explore more of our books and writings. We are confident that they will help you in your financial journey and will be a valuable addition to your financial literacy. Additionally, your feedback means a lot to us. We would be grateful if you could take a moment to leave a review of this guide on the platform from which you have bought the book. Your review will help others to make an informed decision about the book, and it will help us to understand your perspective and improve our future writings.

Lastly, do join us on our Instagram page **@real_anuragyadav** for more financial tips, advice and updates. We would love to hear from you and engage in a meaningful conversation.

Thank you for choosing this guide and we hope you found it informative and helpful. We wish you all the best in your financial journey."

We appreciate your time and hope that you found this guide to be valuable.

Thank you for choosing this guide.

www.ingramcontent.com/pod-product-compliance
Lightning Source LLC
Chambersburg PA
CBHW070841160726
48004CB00001B/458